M000304480

Rules of Engagement

How to Win at Dining with Clients and Other Important People

Revised Edition

Cheryl Walker-Robertson
Certified Protocol and Etiquette Expert

Maturing into adulthood, fine dining was not a topic of discussion nor a priority in my world. My Big Son became an elite athlete in the NBA and I knew then I would be dining at the finest of restaurants more frequently in the company of people who were versed and possessed the skill set of fine dining. This scared me a bit but fortunately I had the opportunity along with family and family members to attend and participate in the fine dining skills workshop with Protocol International led by my friend and expert protocol and etiquette consultant, Cheryl Walker-Robertson. This experience gave me the knowledge and skill set to dine at the finest restaurants with confidence. I recommend this workshop to anyone who is seeking to elevate their fine dining game. A big Thank You to Cheryl and Protocol International for their patience, expertise and guidance!

Tamiyko Prince

There is no substitute for proper etiquette, in fact to be a boss, you need to know all the rules of engagement. This book will give you the prescription for mastering the art of the deal, a must have for your personal and professional toolkit. An amazing read!"

Michelle Taylor-Jones
CEO, The Taylor Group
Author, Poet "Sonnets From My Soul"

I am ecstatic that Cheryl has penned the lessons she shared during the "Refine Your Finer" Luncheon hosted by the Centennial Commission of Zeta Phi Beta Sorority, Inc. Having observed her amazing interaction at two corporate events, I knew she would entertain with finesse while refreshing and refining the etiquette skills of our collegiate to seasoned members. It was the perfect afternoon of laughter mixed with serious conversations that reminded each participant of the importance of speaking through our refined manners while dining. The accolades and stories infused with laughter continue to remind me of how successful the event was THANKS to the unique and expert skills of Cheryl. I plan to share the book with students, corporate coaching clients, Encore Leaders and individuals who understand the pivotal difference of continuing to "refine" their skills.

Jylla Moore Tearte, Ph.D.
20th International President and Centennial Commission Chair
Zeta Phi Beta Sorority, Incorporated
Tearte Family Foundation, COO
EncoreLeadership.com

Rules of Engagement is a must read. We work hard to make sure we have it all together but many times miss the nuance of fine dining. It's is more than which fork to use, it is about how to leverage a dining experience to ensure your guests are served well. Cheryl offers advice in a way that is compelling. She creates a space that is safe and makes one excited about learning and not feel embarrassed because this is something that you ought to have known. Cheryl takes you to the fundamentals that are required to enhance social engagement with others. Kudos to the author for writing a book that represents her many years of experience and expertise. An expertise that reminds us that even with the fast pace (e.g., living with technology) of moving thru life, don't forget the basic skills and protocol required to connect with others in meaningful ways.

Audra Bohannon

©2017 Cheryl Walker-Robertson

This book contains quotations from the following public figures and organizations: Julia Alvarez, Letitia Baldrige, David Beckham, Lois McMaster Bujold, Bennet Cerf, Will Cuppy, T. Harv Ecker, Harvey Mackey, Paul Johnson, Emily Post, and Margaret Walker.

Published in Fort Pierce, Florida by Pipe Publishing, a division of the Stimuknowlogy Institute.

Rules of Engagement may be purchased in bulk for educational, business, fund-raising, or sales promotional use. For information, please email cheryl@4protocol.net

ISBN 978-0-9844475-5-8

Library of Congress Cataloging-In-Publication Data is available.
Cover and Interior Design by Stacey Grainger
Interior Images from Adobe Stock

Dedication

Rules of Engagement is dedicated to the following women in my life:

My mother, Daisy Larcena Walker, my first etiquette instructor.

Linda Spradley Dunn, the ultimate Host, from whom I've learned so much.

Maria Pajil Battle, my mentor, whose guidance, counsel, support and love has meant so much to me.

Odyssey women everywhere, who have given me so many great stories to tell.

"To play the game, you must know the rules. To win, you must know Protocol."

Protocol International

Contents

Foreword

AS social beings, the strength of our relationships relies on the strength of our ability to connect. In a globalized market, connections are forging, more and more, at the dinner table. Whether you are entertaining a business client or meeting your future in-laws for the very first time, a well-played dining experience can be a deal maker or a deal breaker. In the big scheme of interacting with others, small details make a huge impact.

Ask any number of people how long it takes for them to form an opinion of someone they meet for the first time and you will no doubt get many different responses. No matter if the answer is two seconds or sixty, the result is the same. With so many opportunities to engage with others, commanding attention and standing out from among the crowd can seem almost impossible. In all forms of relationships, how you communicate, both verbally and nonverbally, determine how you are perceived. Simply put, impressions matter, and you only have a few seconds to make your mark.

In every game there are rules. Knowing how to execute play by play, with precision, is the difference maker. Dining and entertaining are social experiences, often in a crowded field. To win, you will need a strategy that advances a competitive advantage. Lucky for you, that strategy is in your hands. *Rules of Engagement: How to Win at Dining with Clients and Other Important People* is the premier playbook to coach Game Changers through relationship building with confidence and grace.

Dennis R. Robertson, President
Protocol International's Elite Athletic Division

Introduction

I began to understand and experience the difference between the haves and the have-nots at an early age. I grew up in middle-class America, somewhat a jock, surrounded by lots of boys. My brothers and male cousins were always busy playing interesting games and sports such as kick the can, Mother May I, and H.O.R.S.E. Girly games weren't as much fun to me. Barbie was boring in comparison. So my mother, sensing my *tomboyishness*, insisted I attend etiquette and charm schools. Most of the training took place in upscale hotels or luxury department stores – Strawbridge & Clothier, John Wanamaker's, Lit Brothers. Though not excited by this at the start, it turned out to work to my advantage. Taller than most and athletic, I was chosen along with other participants to model for these stores. Traveling around the city and the Mainline to do shows was a great opportunity. However, compared to other girls in the modeling troupe, I didn't feel quite as confident in navigating some of the social situations that required networking and interacting with the shoppers and dining with the Hosts. I quickly realized even though I could walk with a book on my head, it wasn't quite enough, and I lacked some of the social graces and the interpersonal skills necessary to confidently navigate some of the social situations I found myself in. Consequently, off the runway, I felt awkward. I spent so much time masking my feelings and worried I'd be found out that I would often leave early and not participate as much as I should've to avoid embarrassment. Years later, I was accepted into Harcum Jr. College, in Bryn Mawr, PA on a basketball and volleyball athletic scholarship. Again, on the Mainline, again forced to face the idea that some people seem to operate by a different set of rules, and understood how to navigate their way with people and situations better than others. I certainly could hold my own, thanks to my earlier exposure and experience having attended etiquette and charm schools, but even with that and remembering the old adage "fake it 'til you make it," it was not without a great deal of effort and some pretending to get by. I began to notice the difference between the haves and the have-nots. I'm not talking about money as much as confidence in knowing how to navigate social situations that require a certain knowledge of these unwritten rules.

By the time I graduated college, became a serial entrepreneur and ultimately a flight attendant, it was very clear to me that knowledge of etiquette and protocol were essential life skills. World travel presented challenges and opportunities, both personal and professional...what a game changer! When I first started flying, I would again feel that awkwardness that made me sometimes miss opportunities because of my lack of understanding of the unwritten rules of engagement and fear of embarrassment. Determined to get in the game, I elevated my knowledge, positioned myself for several promotions and received extra training, both formal and informal. The more savvy I became about the game, I knew that more doors would open for me the more I exposed myself to that which was necessary to succeed. It was like learning a new language. Being *Bilingual* took on a whole new meaning, i.e., the language of my native tongue - West Philly and now this new language of the haves. This new language discusses how best to interact with different people in different circumstances requiring different mannerisms, body language, gestures, proximity, eye contact, and yes dining skills.

Etiquette determines how an experience with you at a dining table reflect your values, your ability to take care of someone, and take care of details. In the professional world of business, good manners at the dinner table are equated with competence in business. Knowingly or not, you are measured based on your treatment of other people; how you treat your guests, your waitress and even how you order, is a reflection of how you make decisions. Even a detail like how you season your food at the table can be a reflection of your managerial skills. Having this knowledge, this skill, and knowing this language gave me credibility and offered my relationships the benefits of instant rapport, respect, and trust.

This is what I want for you. In these pages, we will discuss how to navigate the before, during, and after of purposeful business and social interactions over a meal. This knowledge will offer you the behavior, mindset, and language that is impressive, intentional and represents a certain sophistication equal to your values and social savviness.

As a corporate etiquette and protocol expert, my goal is to share with you how to be more powerful, more impressive and more confident. Successfully navigating the social graces associated with dining will afford you the competitive advantage you seek. How you represent yourself is the hallmark of both your business and personal brand.

Whether you are hosting or attending a business dinner, networking with clients or potential customers, or entertaining important people in your life, *"To play the game, you must know the rules. To win, you must know Protocol."*

Your Personal Protocol & Etiquette Coach,
Cheryl Walker-Robertson

1

Pre-Game

Test Your Knowledge

1. Who are your partners for a successful dining experience?

2. What side of the dinner plate will you find your bread and butter plate?

3. When a spoon and/or fork are placed at the top of the plate, for what course are they used?

4. What do you do when asked to pass the salt?

5. What should you do if you will be arriving late to dinner?

6. Is it acceptable to put a small handbag on the table? Your cell phone?

7. When invited to someone's home for dinner, what can you bring?

8. What would you say if you need to leave the table to use the restroom?

9. How do you handle soup that is too hot?

10. At what point in the meal do you offer a toast and who drinks after the toast is offered?

11. What is the formula for negotiating the silverware?

12. Who orders first?

13. How many courses should you order?

14. At what point in the meal should you discuss business?

15. Where should you put your napkin when you temporarily leave the table?

16. What is the silent service code to signal you are resting, rather than finished eating?

17. Is it acceptable to eat in the Continental style in America, today?

18. Is it acceptable to put lipstick on at the table?

19. Who should pay for the bill?

"Etiquette means behaving yourself a little better than is absolutely essential."

Will Cuppy

2

The Anatomy of a Restaurant

Setting Up a Winning Experience

Before we get into the anatomy of a restaurant, let's talk about the logistics of setting up a winning experience for you, your clients and other important people, which is after all *everyone*.

Depending on the type of restaurant you will be dining in, call ahead to make a reservation for you and your guests. Generally, white linen venues will have the option for you to reserve the perfect table for your 'more than a meal' experience. You will want to leave your name and number and inform your contact at the restaurant of the date and time to expect you, and the number of guests. Add these details and the Maître D's name and direct number to your smartphone so you can refer to it quickly when you need it.

During this reservation call, mention the reason for the meal, i.e. important business meeting, meeting the in-laws, proposing marriage, graduation, etc. Make the restaurant, particularly the Maître D, a team member for your success. I recommend you have a favorite restaurant for entertaining where the Maître D, bartender, and waiters know your name. Everyone should have an establishment where when you walk in, there is a personal *Cheers* experience, a restaurant that is happy to see you. When you walk in, you are 'Big Willie' with a favorite table, and they know your favorite drink. There is a sense of familiarity. This will add to your comfort and confidence, and will also be impressive to your guests. Your guests should feel like VIPs when they are with you in *your* restaurant. This is a perfect situation to be at your best.

The day of your meal, arrive early. This is where you and your assistant *should* sweat the seemingly small stuff. The day of your meal, arrive early. If you are the host, survey the section where you and your guests will be dining, to ensure the setup is perfect. Avoid being near a door, the bathroom, the kitchen, or any place where the waiters may gather to gossip. You should wait for all of your guests to arrive. You may want to grab something to drink at the bar or hang in the lobby until they all arrive. Be sure to remind the Maître D of your occasion and to engage in small talk for a short moment.

Key Players in the Anatomy of the Restaurant

In a dining experience, Key Players are the typical people you will need to know. Knowing who they are and their roles and responsibilities you are guaranteed to assure your success as either the host or guest.

The Maître D

The Maître D manages the entire restaurant. Typically, the Maître D is aware of everything happening in the restaurant and is responsible for smooth execution. If you are running late, you will want to call and notify the Maître D. Ask that they accommodate your guests, so they feel special while waiting for your arrival. Be sure to personally give them a nice tip for pitching in to help you send the message that you are in control. The Maître D is your partner. This person should be like a best friend who helps you create a memorable dining experience. Build a professional and friendly relationship with your Maître D in your restaurant.

The Head Waiter is responsible for the success of everything that's happening at your table. They are also the person other Wait Staff takes their directions from during a work shift. Collaborate with the Head Waiter to ensure your experience in the restaurant is amazing.

Use nonverbal cues, like eye contact and slight hand gestures to communicate with your wait staff. It is appropriate to come up with a nod or a look in your eye that communicates, "We are ready for the next course." Or, you may want to signal, "Don't take our order yet, let me get this part of the meeting in before we begin the meal." Keep the communication simple and as nonverbal as possible. You want to be sure that the two of you clearly understand cues. This communication is important, so you and your interaction at the table is polished and politely directive. The Head Waiter or Wait Staff will help you with the pace of the meal and take care of table situations. You and your table's Head Waiter, along with the Wait Staff, manage what happens at your table and therefore the success of the 'not just a meal.'

The Bus Person

In most restaurants, the Bus Person reports to and assists the Head Waiter at your table. This person is the one who clears the table, pours the water, and prepares for the next course to be placed on the table. It is important that you understand the nuances of the bus person's responsibilities. It is not appropriate to ask the bus person for more wine or anything about the meal. This is not their role. If you have questions related to the meal, say to the bus person, "May I see our waiter please." Though this may appear to be a small matter, understanding this role, and the roles of others in the restaurant, reflects your ability to navigate situations appropriately. This also demonstrates your awareness of the chain of command and restaurant protocol.

The Sommelier

Also known as the wine steward, the Sommelier helps to create the wine list, takes care of the wine inventory, and recommends wine to customers, according to their tastes and the meal they have chosen. The sommelier can also pour the wine.

The Bartender

There may be times when you will entertain guests for a *meet and greet* prior to your meal. When appropriate, the bar area is a great location for entertaining in this situation. You may even want to suggest, for example, dinner reservations at 7 pm and a brief *meet and greet* for a cocktail at the bar at 6:15 pm.

Get to know the Bartender. The bar is where you will order liquor, like Jack Daniels or Cosmopolitan. These are not the type drinks that pair well with a meal and not advised to order during the meal. Beer or wine (white or red) are the types of drinks you would order with a meal. When you order a pre-dinner drink, finish it and pay for it at the bar. If you do order a glass of wine from the bar and want to finish it with your meal or at the table, ask the bartender to arrange to have it brought to you at your table. This is so you don't walk through the restaurant carrying a glass of wine in your hand. Try to keep the bar area experience and meal separate. Pay and tip the bartender before leaving the bar. A 10-15% tip is appropriate. Remember in protocol and etiquette, small details matter.

The Coat Check Person

In fine dining situations, make sure you check extra outerwear and extra accessories. These items are checked with the Coat Check person. When you use this service, tip the person who handles these items for you and your guests. A dollar or two is an appropriate tip for each item. If the restaurant does not have an identified Coat Check person, you may want to leave a tip for the restaurant Maitre D to take care of everything. Another opportunity to be 'Big Willie' is to accommodate and 'wow' everyone.

Meet and greet your guests and have their coats, etc. taken to the coat check area. This is part of the experience of taking great care of your guests. Avoid going to your table with coats, umbrellas, big bags, or unnecessary items in your hands. Women who carry huge purses should have a smaller purse that fits into the larger bag. Before heading to the table, remove the smaller, dainty purse and check the larger one.

The Restroom Attendant

Not all venues will have a Restroom Attendant. Depending on the restaurant, the Restroom Attendant services the restrooms and ensures guests have the toiletries they need. If you or your guests have an emergency, like a spill, a loose hem, a tear in hosiery, a stain on your tie, or similar mishaps, the restroom attendant may be able to assist in resolving issues rather quickly.

The Chef

Just like the Maître D manages everything that's happening in the *front of the house*, as they say, in the *back of the house* there is the Chef. The Chef controls everything that happens in the kitchen. They manage all of the specialists, all of the food prep and have a tough job to juggle. This person, along with their staff, takes responsibility for the accurate preparation, temperature and presentation of your meal, especially when specialty items are ordered.

If you frequent a restaurant often and have a great relationship with staff, depending on the restaurant, you may want to ask if the Chef will make a brief, special appearance to your table. Imagine if you were to whisper to the Maître D, since you have built great rapport, "Can we have the Chef come out to say hello to my clients?" Wow! A famous Chef comes out to greet your table. What a nice touch. This type of attention is generally reserved for frequent visitors who have a personal, but professional relationship with the restaurant.

The Valet Attendant

There may be any number of reasons why you would choose to valet park, rather than use the self-parking area. Keep in mind there are restaurants that only provide valet parking, and self-parking is not an option. In either case, the valet plays an important role in the overall dining experience that is hosted by you. Really impress your guests. Let them know that you will be taking care of the valet tab and to mention your name or your company's name when they pull up at the Valet. This can be done discretely by simply giving the Lead Valet Attendant your name, the company name and the name, of your guests and/or a description of their car. Pay the Attendant and tip in advance.

Key Protocol and Etiquette Plays:

- Familiarize yourself with the layout of the restaurant before guests arrive.

- Frequent the same restaurants for the familiarity factor, it's a source of confidence.

- Select the best table considering your objective. For example, because you will be conducting business in addition to the meal, you may want to be away from high traffic areas, loud music, and any distractions. General rule, avoid tables near the door, kitchen, bar, and restrooms.

The Play:

The Bank is receiving an Award at the industry's Annual Black Tie Gala. You land one of the coveted tickets and are sitting with the two Sr. VP's, the Chief Diversity Officer, Chief Marketing Officer, the President of the company's ad agency, and one of your business clients. In front of each of you are four knives, five forks, two spoons, four stems and two plates. You are hungry and thirsty, and no one has touched the rolls nor the water glass. You are thinking "I am about to break the ice" and reach for the water glass on the left...

Your Move:

Understand the layout of your place setting so that everyone follows your lead. Remember this easy hint. **BMW**= **Bread** *on your far left;* **Meal** *in the center; and* **Water** *glass on your right.*

"Nothing is less important than
which fork you use.
Etiquette is the science of living.
It embraces everything.
It is ethics. It is honor."

Emily Post

3

The Anatomy of a Place Setting

Customarily, you won't have nearly as many utensils at a home table display or in a restaurant as demonstrated in this section. However, when attending a banquet, gala, or special event like a wedding, table settings can be overwhelming and intimidating to maneuver. So, let's go play by play and confer on what to expect.

Always work from the outside in when picking up utensils. Notice tableware for liquids are on the right, tableware for solids are on the left. This tip helps you to understand which water glass is yours and which bread plate is theirs. If you reach for the water glass on the left, oops!

The flatware, also known as silverware, on the right of the plate indicates what courses you'll be served and whether or not you will have soup or shrimp cocktail. Flatware on the left indicate if your salad will be served before or after your meal. You can anticipate so much based on the way the table is set. There are a variety of courses - nuts, appetizer, soup, entrée, salad, cheese, and dessert. You will, for the most part, know by the table setting and the amount of silverware set what courses to expect. Knowing what to expect and being familiar with a table setting will give you confidence and the ability to pay attention to your fellow diners for conversation and rapport building, instead of trying to follow someone's lead because you don't know. Awkward and distracting. You want to be known for who you are and what you have to say rather than being known for starting the ripple effect of everyone using the wrong water glass.

If dining American, the salad fork will be to the far left of the setting. When dining Continental, the salad fork will be closest to your plate, indicating salad is served after the main course. In these settings, the salad is served last as a palate cleanser in transition from the main meal to the dessert. Confused yet? The story goes that here in America, we became so impatient about waiting for our meal. Someone got the grand idea to start serving the salad first. If you travel internationally, you will often see the salad fork as the last utensil instead of the first.

Formal Dinner Place Setting

1 Bread plate			17 Salad knife
2 Butter knife	7 Red wine glass	12 Salad fork	18 Meat knife
3 Cake fork	8 White wine glass	13 Dinner fork	19 Fish knife
4 Cake spoon	9 Sherry glass	14 Dessert fork	20 Dinner spoon
5 Water goblet	10 Place card	15 Salad plate	21 Soup spoon
6 Champagne goblet	11 Napkin	16 Service plate	22 Seafood fork

Knives are always turned inward with the blades towards the plate. The historical rationale is, if the blades are turned inside, they wouldn't be used as weapons. There is a lot of historical reference to this practice and some pretty good stories as well. Cardinal Richelieu is said to be responsible for the ruling that the tips of all knives brought to the table must be blunted. Ostensibly, this discouraged diners from using their knives to pick their teeth, but there had been more than a few problems with diners picking on one another.

There is a fork for every knife. Forks are on the left and Knives are on the right. There may be one fork at the top of the table setting and if having a shrimp cocktail, the appropriate fork will sit inside a spoon to the far right.

Pay close attention to details like this and understand why the table arrangements look the way they do. Also important to note, once you use a utensil it should never go back on the clean linen. It should be taken away with the dinnerware or placed appropriately on your plate. In some establishments, they will ask you to keep your knife and sometimes even your fork to keep from having to wash so many utensils.

The Play:

Panicked, Mr. Baker calls the famous Chinese restaurant he always chooses. It has rich history, the food is great, there's always the potential to see a celebrity or two, and they have a table there with his name on it. Mr. Baker calls the Maître D, who informs him the client arrived early and is in the restaurant foyer awaiting his arrival, slightly star struck. Baker and the Maître D devise a plan to give the client a tour of the restaurant, introduce him to anyone famous in the restaurant, tell him a few good stories, then take him to the table where they will be seated. The plan is worthy of the generous tip he gives the Maître D.

Your Move:

Don't be late. Take traffic into consideration. Tip the Maître D' $20 for saving your day. Note the benefits of being familiar with the restaurant where you entertain.

Glassware

Glassware, also known as stemware, is placed on the right side of the table setting. Sometimes all the options for what you may drink will be on the table, sometimes it is brought to the table as you order. It is important to know either way. Raise your right hand, yes really raise it now - know that is the side of the table setting for your glassware - your water glass, wine - red and white, champagne, iced tea, etc. Hold red wine glasses by the bowl. Hold white wine and champagne glasses by the stem to keep what's inside the glass from getting prematurely warm due to your body temperature.

The dessert utensils are placed at the top of your place setting in a formal place setting. To prepare for dessert, once everything else is cleared, you will do what's called a "pull down." To execute properly, pull the fork to the left and the spoon to the right of where your dessert plate will be to prepare for dessert. Often instead, when it's time for dessert, Wait Staff will either do the honors for you or they will bring the appropriate utensil based on your order. If you are having a bowl of ice cream, you use the spoon, if you are having cake you would use the fork.

Do's and Don'ts

- Never turn your stemware upside down on the table. Some folks think this is a good way to inform the Waiter that you don't want wine. The best way is to lightly tap the rim of the glass when the wine is being poured. The Waiter or the Sommelier will understand - *another silent service code.*

- Do always pass the salt and pepper together, they are married.

- Remember solids on the left and liquids on the right.

"Keeping the sharp part pointed toward yourself is the least you can do as a show of faith that no matter how provocative your fellow diners may turn out to be, you, at least, are willing to let them live until dessert.'

Miss Manners."

4

napkin management

The way you handle your dining manners may send a message as to how competent you are at handling your business. Napkin management is another one of those giveaways.

In a formal situation, and when there is one, wait for the Guest of Honor to pick up their napkin before you pick up your own. In not so formal situations, the moment you are seated, properly fold your napkin, in half and place in your lap. Typically, your napkin is placed to the left of the table setting. The fold of napkin should be facing your waist, with the flap facing your knees. This permits you to easily wipe your hands or fingers inside the napkin. If you soil the top of your napkin, flip it over to expose a clean section. With this strategy, your napkin appears clean throughout dinner.

Folding your napkin in half with the flap facing your knees also serves another purpose. If you have to excuse yourself to the restroom, place the napkin on your seat. You don't want a dirty napkin face side up for your guests to see. Nor do you want it to leave the residue of food in the seat where you are returning to sit. When you do leave the table, push your chair in under the table as not to obstruct the walk around area for the wait staff and other diners.

At the end of the meal, watch the host at your table. When he or she places their napkin back on the table, to the left of the place setting not too neatly folded, yet not without care, this usually signals that the meal is complete. At this time, everyone can place their napkins on the table in the same manner.

One last tidbit about napkins: Depending on the color of clothing you and guests wear to dinner, you may want to ask the waiter to exchange white napkins for black napkins. White napkins will often leave white shavings from the linen cloth on your clothing. You can politely say, "Excuse me, could you replace all our napkins with black napkins?" *Small detail, huge impact.* Your guests will remember you for it!

Key Plays:

- Place napkin in your seat if you need to excuse yourself from the table at any time during dinner.

- If you accidentally drop your napkin on the floor, ask the wait staff for another one. Do not pick a napkin up from the floor and continue to use it, unless you're in someone's home. Then do pick it up.

- The napkin is always placed to the left of the place setting. It is the silent service code that the meal is completed. If you are the host, place your loosely folded napkin to the left of your place setting and stand. If you are a guest, graciously use the napkin to tap around your mouth and place your napkin to the left of your plate.

"When people talk about political correctness, the only element of any value is good manners."

Paul Johnson

5

Bread and Butter

Do's and Don'ts

- Do choose a roll from the basket and pass counter-clockwise, *to the right.*

- Don't butter your entire roll once you have it.

- Do add your pat of butter from the foil or from the community dish onto to your bread plate. Never butter your roll from the community butter dish.

- Don't take one huge bite from your buttered roll.

- Do break off a bite-sized piece of your roll and butter just that small piece from your bread plate.

- Don't get filled up by scarfing down 5 rolls before you order, no matter how hungry you are.

"A stunning first impression was not the same thing as love at first sight. But surely it was an invitation to consider the matter."

Lois McMaster Bujold

CHAPTER

6

Ordering

Cocktails

When at the bar order a cocktail, a pre-dinner drink. Finish it at the bar. When at the table order a drink that is suitable for pairing with your meal. I mentioned this detail a little earlier but feel it's also important to mention again here. Be mindful that you order an appropriate drink meant to pair well with the meal at the dinner table. Don't order a Jack Daniel with dinner. Consume your cocktails before the meal or after.

At the dinner table with your meal, order beer, red or white wine with your meal. There are so many varieties of both beer and wine to choose from. Some experts say you can't go wrong with a Chardonnay or Pinot Grigio white wine with poultry, salad, or fish. A Merlot, Cabernet, or

Malbec with red meats and wild game is appropriate. If you have a spicy food choice, a great beer may be appropriate as a beverage. A Belgian or India Pale Ale (IPA) are frequent selections for the beer connoisseur. It's contemporary to have it your way - you can choose light and easy, red with white meat, and a robust white with red meat depending on your taste and preference. Your Waiter and, if available, the restaurant Sommelier are able to make great suggestions for pairing. Otherwise tea, lemonade are always appropriate. These beverages are often served unsweetened. You'll have to add a sweetener from the package. When doing so, fold the packages after they are empty and tuck them under your plate to keep the table neat.

The Play:

At the quarterly meeting with her Sorors, Sharon made reservations for eight at the Highlawn Pavilion, a 5-Star, white linen restaurant that some of the Sorors had not yet been to. Soon after all the preliminaries, the Waiter approaches the table to take everyone's order. First two Sorors very decidedly and swiftly place their orders. Once the Waiter asks Sandy for her order, she proceeds to ask him a series of questions.

- "How do you cook your veggies?"
- "Does the sauce contain fish or other animal ingredients?"
- "Do you have soy milk?"
- "Is your marinara sauce made with chicken stock?"
- "What's in the soup?"

Sharon saw every Soror either look at their watch or roll their eyes while waiting to order. The Waiter's eyes looked glazed over as well.

Your Move:

As host, and informed of Sandy's diet, Sharon should ask for best suggestions for Sandy's meal in advance. This way, Sandy would have known her options and not hold up the order for the entire table. As guest, Sandy could also call ahead and decide meal plans with the help of the restaurant.

From the Menu

When you are entertaining a small or large group, you may want to keep two things in mind - Dietary restrictions and your budget. Be sure to ask your guests about any dietary restrictions in advanced. Part of your role as Host of your special needs. Your role as Guest is to inform the Host so that there is no awkwardness for you, for the restaurant, or for the group. A winning protocol tip is to call ahead for this line of questioning or simply let the restaurant know you are a Vegan. Ask what would they suggest you order, this way you know in advance.

A winning group strategy for a budget-minded meal, given ample time, is to have the restaurant print a special menu for you with only what you are offering, translation - *willing to pay for.* For example, ask your favorite restaurant to customize a menu with all the items within your price range. Give your guests options: soup or salad, chicken parmesan or sesame ginger salmon, a vegetarian choice, and two options for dessert. Consult with the restaurant Sommelier on which wines to choose within your budget that also pair with your menu. This way you control the budget and your guests are impressed by the branded menu. This is also a winning idea for family functions hosted in restaurants.

The Play:

Although not in the small company's budget, the company's CEO decide to take a chance and travel to meet a potential corporate client and bring along and a new Representative. The plan was to fly in, have the meeting, and fly out the same day. When they arrive, the prospect calls to apologize for her tardiness. Her previous meeting was longer than she expected so suggests a dinner meeting at a fancy restaurant close by instead. This could mean an overnight stay for the small company. Not in the budget, but the business owner wants the business and would like to 'save face'.

Upon seating, the Waiter asks for drink orders. The client orders a modest Chardonnay, the business owner orders a modest Cabernet, the new Representative orders a Remy Martin "double please". The prospect suggests we place the dinner order in the interest of time. She orders the Salmon; the business owner orders Salmon too; and the new Representative orders the Lobster Surf and Turf,"Well done please".

The business owner discovers the values, lack of judgement, and the personality of the new Representative at the dinner table. This will be the 'last meal' for the new Representative, who is clearly not a good fit for the ambitious small company.

There will be times when you will not be able to customize a menu, or it may not be appropriate. Another winning strategy as Host is to casually discuss the menu and offer recommendations. This signals to your guests that you would like them to stay within the price range of the items you recommend. You may say to your guests, "This restaurant is fantastic and is known for its prime rib. The Chilean sea bass is also amazing. Making these recommendations is not only a suggestion for what is tasty, it's also a cue to ensure your choices stay within the price range of the sea bass and the prime rib. People who understand protocol and etiquette will get it. Those that don't will blow your budget and also blow their cover.

Some Other Ordering Do's and Don'ts

- Do order a meal easy to eat. Remember this is about your relationship, your brand, the impression you leave, and not as much about how good the spaghetti sounds.

- Don't order finger foods - juicy cheeseburger, crabs, fried chicken, or lobster. Order foods that you won't need three napkins and a bib to get through the meal.

- Do order the same number of courses as everyone else. This is about pace.

- Don't take forever to order. This could imply you are indecisive. Assess, analyze, and decide. Then be confident in your decision.

- Do ask a few questions or ask the Waiters opinion. They really do have one and it's valuable. It's also a great way to engage your waiter.

- Do, as the Host, order last, allowing the guests to go first. This is one of many cues, to the Waiter as to who they should take direction from at the table. The relationship between Waiter and Host is an important one, so establish your role early - greeting, seating, ordering. When you take control, the Waiter knows to take signals from you on timing, pace, table needs, and success. If something is wrong or something is happening, and they need to inform just one person at the table, they know to come to you. Also, of course, they know who to bring the check to at the end of the meal. Another protocol and etiquette rule is if you do the inviting you do the paying.

The Play:

Ed is a well-dressed, popular leader in the organization. He is well respected and fun to be around. He has won the Salesman of the Year award, a sought after trophy that includes special recognition from the CEO, other execs, and peers. Everyone arrives excited and finds their seats by table number. Ed is sitting at table number one with the CEO. The CEO is looking forward to table talk with the top salesperson in his company.

The first course is soup. Ed proceeds to eat immediately upon being served, not waiting for the grace to be said, not waiting for the cue from the table's host, the CEO. The CEO glares over at him then back to the podium where the chosen person says a blessing. Next service is salad. Wait staff is coming around to collect the soup bowls. Ed prematurely hands the bowl to the Waiter without looking up at her. As the salads are served, once again Ed starts eating without waiting for everyone to be served first. He grabs the fork like a spear and chases the cherry tomato around on his plate, stabbing at it before picking it up with his hand. There is no conversation at the table, just the awkward glances. Ed finally picks his head up from the entree to say something profound to the CEO, but all the company's founder could see was food in Ed's mouth as he spoke. The CEO has lost his appetite. At the end of the meal, he presents Ed with the award and a bonus. The next day he calls HR to insist all salespeople in the company complete a dining skills course on how to entertain a client over a meal.

Your Move:

The truth is we don't know what we don't know. When we are great at big tasks, an understanding of the rules of engagement at the dinner table may seem small. Dining in business and social environments not only speak to your manners, upbringing, and your exposure, but also to your professionalism, judgement, and training. We often associate competence with table manners. The message you send stretches way beyond the table.

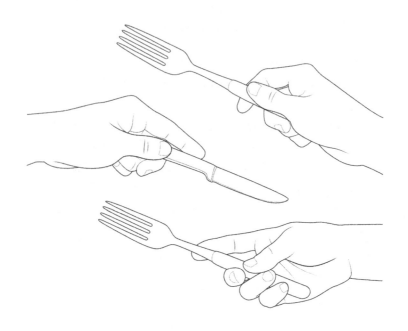

Handling your utensils (pun intended)

The way you handle your utensils can be a giveaway - that you are a sagacious diner that is competent, or an ill-informed, inexperienced diner that is not. To handle utensils with etiquette, put the butt of the utensils in the center of your palms. Place the fork in your left hand, knife in your right. The index finger should be at the top of the handle of each utensil. Avoid placing your finger on the head of the fork or blade of the knife, so gravy and other sauces don't soil your fingers or worse, your knuckles.

The index finger is mostly straight and rests near the base of the top of the utensil. The other four fingers wrap around the handles. While your index finger is resting on the top, your thumb juxtaposes it on the side. The end of the handles should be touching the base of your palm. This is the same beginning in both American and Continental styles.

If dining American style, hold the fork and knife the same way, but after cutting one or two small bite sized sections of food, you place your knife diagonally across the top of your plate. Flip your fork to your right hand with tines up, pick up what you've cut and convey to your mouth tines up. Continue in this pattern to put the fork back in your left hand; pick the knife up again; cut one or two more pieces; put the knife down; and put the fork back over to your right hand. Your free hand, typically your left, is in your lap. This can be an involved and encumbering process.

In Continental style dining, you will keep the fork in your left hand and the knife in your right. Use the knife to cut and push the food onto and on top of the fork. The fork tines should be turned down, food conveyed to your mouth tines down. You hold the utensils in your hand, wrists above the table until you've finished or indicate with your silverware that you are resting.

Only take bite size cuts. Never cut up all your food and then eat. That is considered improper in fine dining and typically a strategy designed for people under 7 years old.

Silent Service Codes

In the restaurant business, a plate is discussed in relation to the time on a clock. For example, 12 is at the top of the plate, 6 is at the bottom, 3 is at the far right, and the 9 is at the far left.

America Style - When you are finished with your meal, place your knife and your fork together, *fork tines up* to indicate 10:20 on your plate. Meaning your utensils are diagonal across your plate. This tells the server that you are finished, and they can clear your plate.

If you want to talk, or when resting, place your fork in the diagonal position and your knife at the top of the plate.

Continental Style - If you want to talk, or when resting, place your fork and knife in an "X" like formation on top of your plate with the fork tines down. This communicates to the Waiter that you are not finished with your meal. Not to take your plate away. When you are finished with a meal, place utensils together at the 10:20 position with fork tines down. This is the silent code that indicates to your Waiter that the meal is complete.

It is important to know whether or not to place utensils facing up or down on the plate. For American dining, place utensils facing up. When dining Continental style, place utensils facing down. Be consistent throughout your meal. Either you chose to dine American style or the Continental style. Be decisive in your selection of style. Note, most people prefer Continental dining because this winning protocol is easier to navigate and lacks the cumbersome business of back and forth with the American style. Either way, be consistent.

Key Plays:

- Keep hands above the table when dining Continental.

- Keep your free hand in your lap when dining American.

- Be consistent throughout the meal whether dining American or Continental.

- How you hold your utensils is a giveaway as to your style, your etiquette, and your protocol acumen.

The Play:

Dennis, President of Protocol International's Elite Athlete Division has set up a dinner meeting with a top tier high school athlete and his AAU coach. Dennis wears his uniform of slacks, custom white shirt with cufflinks, and sports coat. The Coach shows up in a workout sweat suit, while the player arrives in hanging mid-thigh jeans and a hoodie. Regretting they were not at TGI Fridays, Dennis asks his guests to order what they want. The Coach orders the most expensive item on the menu, so does the athlete. The Coach orders another meal as a 'doggy bag' to go, and so does the athlete.

Dennis graciously hosts the meal, making sure both men enjoy themselves and that their every need is met. While discussing sports and the young athlete's career on and off the court, Dennis shares real life stories and discusses the importance of protocol and etiquette. He discusses the importance of being a leader and not a follower, and that the athlete should understand the off-court rules of the game - his values, his image, and who and what he represents.

Needless-to-say, Dennis now offers quarterly Protocol training to the whole AAU team - all ages, coaches, and parents.

Your Move:

As adults and leaders in the lives of young people, we are role models. Presence is a powerful word and a powerful play for business people and coaches, on and off the courts - sports and life. Who do you represent? How do you represent? There is room for improvement for each of us - whether we are MVP's or most improved.

Host Duties

In Protocol, everyone has a role. At the dining table, there's the role of the Guest, the role of the Host, and sometimes the role of a Guest of Honor.

If you are the Host, you are responsible for everything that happens at the table, and you are responsible for ensuring that the goals and objectives of the meal are met and that everyone is having a good time in the time allotted. You must pay attention to everyone and everything.

As the Guest of Honor, the occasion is all about you. Guests attend the event to celebrate you. When you are the Guest of Honor, Guests follow your lead to start the meal and to signal when the meal is over. When you pick up the napkin, Guests know it is time to pick up their napkin. When you pick up a drink, Guests know it is okay to drink. As you begin to eat, everyone else knows it is time to eat. This role is especially observed in extremely formal events, but can also be applied when you're casually hosting a group of people to honor someone.

When you are the Guest, your responsibility is to enjoy yourself and add to a good time not detract from it. You should not highlight anything negative about the food, the people, or the circumstances. Your interaction is about the relationships. But what if the food is not edible as cooked? If you have an undercooked steak, you may want to send it back depending on the circumstances, conversation, or relationship between you and Guests. But if the steak comes back and it's still not good, don't return it a second or third time. Enjoy the company and eat the other items on your plate. A word of caution: Don't make the dinner date about the steak and cause everyone to focus on you and your unfortunate meal. Your role is to have a good time and not to cause any kind of issue that make others feel bad because you had a bad experience.

Business Lunch or Dinner in the Home

Seating arrangements are made by the Host. It is never appropriate for Guests to shift name cards or take a seat at a table other than the one to which they have been assigned. It is the Host's prerogative to decide how to seat Guests.

When entertaining business associates at home, the *head seats,* at either end of the table, are taken by the Host and Hostess.

At a round or square table, the head seat is wherever the Host wants to sit. At a rectangular table, the head seats are at the ends of the table. The most important Guests occupy the right-hand seats, while the second most important Guests, if any, occupy the left-hand seats.

Unless protocol is being observed, other Guests should not be seated according to their importance. If protocol is being observed, everyone present should understands the seating arrangements.

At a business lunch or dinner where spouses are not present, Guests are more likely to be seated in accordance with their importance.

The Play:

Members of the honor society from your alma mater are meeting over a meal. As the Host, you suggest everyone meet at the bar and then you can be seated once all have arrived. Jane ordered a double and is now trying to make her way across the restaurant with this drink in her left hand, her big purse in her right, and in heels that now seem too tight for her. The table now feels so, so far away.

Alleviate the need for your guests to balance her belongings while walking through the crowded restaurant. Ask the Bartender or Hostess to please ensure the drinks for guests are carried to your table. An important note, it is best to finish bar drinks (cocktails) at the bar and then transition to dinner drinks (wine, beer) for the meal at the table. Another good play here is to leave the big purse in your car or check it at the Hostess station. A dainty purse is much more presentable for a dinner date anyway.

The Guest of Honor is seated to the right of the Host, with a second Guest of Honor seated to the left. Less important Guests are arranged, often according to rank, around the table.

Place Cards

Place cards are appropriate when entertaining 8 or more Guests joining you for lunch or dinner. They are a great idea because Guests can see where they are requested to sit without direction from the Host. Place Cards can lie flat, or be positioned to stand up. The Place Card can be set on top of the napkin, in the middle of the plate, above the forks just above the plate, or lean against the stemware. If the event is informal and everyone knows one another, you can write first names only, distinguishing Guests who may share the same name. If the event is formal, use full names and honorifics. It would lack protocol not to include one's rank or title.

Cups and Saucers

Cups and saucers are served to the right, but not until coffee or tea is served.

Key Plays:

- As a Host, remember that the goals and objectives of the meal are always important. See that they are met.

- As a Guest, thank your Host and compliment the choice of venue and meal. Depending on the nature of the dinner, a handwritten note is always special. Order some personal stationary today.

- When invited, someone with protocol and etiquette always arrives with a gift. Appropriate gifts are music, candy, wine or champagne, candles, or something suitable to celebrate the occasion.

- The Host gives the signal that Guests follow in moving from one course of the meal to the next.

"Manners make the world work. They're not only based on kindness but also efficiency. When people know what to do, the world is smoother. When no one knows what to do, it's chaos."

Letitia Baldrige

7

Body Language at the Table

There is power in all communication, including nonverbal communication. In many ways, body language communicates what you think and feel emotionally. It is important to convey a message of confidence, warmth, and professionalism.

One of the most common faux pas during formal and informal dining is elbows on the dinner table. Although the etiquette rule is that you can put your elbows on the table between courses, most people become overly relaxed when doing so. I highly recommend to my clients to reframe from the practice. Why lose ground after you have been intentional about the details up to this point.

Like elbows on the table, leaning back in your chair will also score you a technical foul. Your entire body should squarely face the table, and your feet should be flat on the floor. The space between your back and the back of the chair should form an imaginary "V' shape. If you are not comfortable sitting upright in this way; practice, practice, and practice. Not only does sitting in this form relay the message that you are attentive and interested in your Guests, but it is also great posture.

The next time you are in a restaurant, take a moment to scan the room and assess the way people are sitting and what their body language expresses. What do you interpret from their posture? Just as you make assumptions about others based on their posture, people make assumptions about yours as well. Are you engaged, excited, bored, tired, too casual, like the company you are in, or not? Check your body language and what it communicates.

Key Plays:

- Posture that reflects your attentiveness and interest is not just for the dinner table. Attune to informal body language during meetings and in general business affairs.

- Good eye contact also conveys a sense of attentiveness.

- Keep your mobile phone off the table and out of site. If you must have a phone in the case of a unique emergency, be sure your phone is on vibrate. Even in this mode, the phone can be a distraction. The volume or the intensity of the vibration should be minimal.

"Friends and good
manners will carry you
where money won't go."

Margaret Walker

8

The Toast

Raise Your Glass...

A toast is an easy and special way to acknowledge a Guest or Guests. Sometimes a Guest will toast to the Host. If you are the Host being toasted, it is proper etiquette not take a drink. For example, if the Guest says, "So here's to Cheryl Walker-Robertson, for an amazing dining skills class. We're so grateful for learning so much from her, and we will be forever indebted to her for being impressive when we dine with our clients and other important people. Here's to Cheryl." Everyone raises their glass. I will raise my glass, but not take a drink.

The protocol of returning a toast...

In return, I might say, "Here's to having an amazing table of friends who are open and loving enough and gracious enough to enjoy this workshop and make it fun. May all of your dining experiences be as good as this one. Here's to you." After this statement, we all drink from our glasses. A toast should be sincere, complimentary, short and fun. Depending on how formal the situation is, you may want to stand to toast. However, toasts are also appropriate if everyone is seated. In either case, be brief, be seated, and begin the meal.

Raise the Glass

A lot of people think a toast consists of touching glasses. The contemporary rule around toasting says it is not appropriate to touch glasses, however most people do not know the contemporary rule. The proper etiquette, in this case, is to be considerate enough to break protocol and click glasses. In this scenario, "When in Rome, do as the Romans do."

Key Plays:

- Keep toasts short. A toast is not intended to be a long monologue. We don't want anyone's arm to fall off waiting for you to finish a toast.

- Your toast should be relevant. It should reflect the importance, joy, or reverence of the situation.

- Be sure to give everyone participating in the toast eye contact. End the toast with a focus on the person to whom the toast is given.

"*Good manners:
The noise you don't
make when you're
eating soup.*"

Bennet Cerf

Paying the Bill and Tips

End of Meal Protocol

It is customary to walk your Guests to the door of the restaurant and thank them for their attendance. This is not the time to bring up new business, but a brief moment to solidify the relationship you have built over dinner. A firm handshake and a sincere thank you will do. If coats or belongings were left with at the coat check, be sure Guests retrieve them. When valet service has been used, remind Guests that you have taken care of them.

The protocol of the check

If you have not made prior arrangements with the restaurant, request the check after coffee or dessert is served, depending on the meal. Quickly review the numbers and settle the bill. It is not appropriate to dispute the accuracy of a check in the company of your Guest. Only after you have escorted all your Guests to the door and said your goodbyes, should you speak with restaurant staff about a discrepancy you would like to question.

Tips

There is an acronym for TIPS, "To Insure Proper Service." Traditionally, tips are a way to recognize great service and to supplement the income of those who serve you. It is important to keep this in mind as you patronize different venues. Staff is expected to provide great service, and in return, you are expected to leave a great tip.

Who Receives a Tip?

Maître D

Unless you need the Maître D for a special favor or request, it may not be necessary to tip this person. However, when you use this service, again, depending on the request, you should budget between $10 and $20 for the Maître D. For example, you are late. You call them to say, "Dr. Smith is on the way, this is what she looks like, and this is what she will be driving. Please take care of her. Have her have a seat at the bar. Give her whatever she wants. Make sure she orders an appetizer because I'm going to need a little more time getting there. Please check on her once after you see her, just to make sure she's okay and I will take care of you when I get there."

Waiter

The Waiter and the bus person share a tip. Sometimes this includes more than the people waiting on your table. At some restaurants, everyone on the shift shares a tip. As I mentioned earlier, the restaurant staff depend on tips to supplement their salary. They basically survive on tips because their base salaries are minimum wages or less. When you receive great service, you want to give a 20% tip. If the service is fantastic, leave more. Only leave a 15% tip when the service was just okay, nothing spectacular. This is considered as a basic tip.

Restroom Attendant

It is a courtesy to leave the Restroom Attendant $1 if you visit this area. In the event they assist you with an unexpected problem, spot removal, spared a safety pin, or helped mend a failing hem, for example, then it is appropriate to tip $3 to $5.

Depending on the exclusiveness of the venue, Valet Attendants typically expect between a $3 and $5 tip. Again, the more exclusive the venue, the more I tend to tip. I also consider whether I am settling the valet service ticket for additional Guests. Big tippers get treated very well. This goes without saying, but the service staff will always appreciate big tippers. When you frequent a familiar restaurant, build a relationship with staff and tip well, they can't wait for you to return and will mince words over who will be serving you.

Key Plays:

- As the Host, you should make arrangements to take care of the tips. Include this expense in your initial budget.

- Present your credit card to the Waiter or Maître D before Guests arrive, to ensure a bill does not come to the table. This also avoids the debate over who should pay for the meal.

- If you frequent a restaurant, your tip is very important. This becomes part of your personal and professional brand. You really want everyone in the restaurant to be happy to wait on you and your Guests. Extra benefits come with being a great tipper.

"They don't teach etiquette much anymore, but if you ever have to choose between incredibly advanced accounting for overachievers and remedial knife and fork, head for the silverware."

Harvey Mackey

10

Styles of Dining

Fast Food

These are quick serve restaurants that focus on convenience, low prices, and obviously speed. Fast food restaurants are the most familiar type of dining for most people. Although health observers criticize these venues, until there are changes in subsidies from animal agriculture to organic farming, we probably won't be seeing many vegan fast food restaurants.

Fast Casual

Fast food casual has become quite a trend in the restaurant industry. These venues are a bit more upscale and more expensive than fast food. These restaurants may offer disposable dishes and flatware, but the food is usually more upscale and made with better ingredients than the typical fast food restaurant. Open kitchens, where you can see your food prepared, are popular fast casual restaurants.

Buffet

All you can eat! This is a favorite kind of dining for many people, especially if they have a big appetite and the goal is to satisfy hunger. Appeals to buffets are the self-serve and no wait features.

Café

Sometimes called a bistro, these restaurants don't offer table service. You order food at the counter and seat yourself. Menu items can be simple, like coffee and sandwiches, and can range up to full entrees. Cafés often have an intimate and relaxed atmosphere. Outdoor seating is also a trademark of the café.

Family Style

This type of dining provides waited table service, but the food is brought out on large platters. Guests share portions from the platter, serving themselves. Family style dining is more common in Asian restaurants.

Casual

This kind of full-service dining offers full table service in a relaxed environment. Casual dining typically has a bigger menu and are more moderately priced. They often serve alcohol or have a full-service bar.

Fine

Think valet service and well-groomed servers in uniforms and white linen service. Fine dining, as the name implies, offers the finest in quality, service, and atmosphere. The prices will also reflect the quality. These restaurants are usually unique in their menu and restaurant design. Most fine dining restaurants also serve vegan options.

Butler Service

Food is presented on trays, from the left of the guest, by servers. Utensils are available for seated guests to serve themselves. This is also used for butler passed hors d'oeuvres at réceptions.

Russian (Silver) Service

Food is cooked tableside, like cart French service, except servers put the foods on platters and then pass the platters at tableside. Guests help themselves to the food and assemble their plates. Service is from the left, while French cart service and Russian service both prepare food tableside. In Russian service, the food is served on platters for the Guests to make their selection. Butler and Russian service allow Guests to select their food from a platter, but the platters are assembled in the kitchen for butler and tableside for Russian.

In these type atmospheres, the most important thing is for the planner and the caterer to have the same understanding. The planner should also know that these styles take more time and usually cost more.

Reception Service

Light foods are served and displayed buffet-style on a table. Guests usually stand and serve themselves. They normally do not sit down to eat. These types of events are sometimes referred to as a "walk and talk." Finger food and fork food are served. It is inappropriate to serve food that requires a knife or is difficult to eat while standing.

Butler Hors d'oeuvres Service

Food is put on trays in the kitchen and passed by servers. Guests serve themselves, using cocktail napkins provided by the server. This is a typical style of service used for upscale receptions. This style of service is only appropriate for "finger food."

Action Stations

Action stations are similar to a buffet. Chefs prepare and serve food at the buffet (rather than in the kitchen). Foods that lend themselves well to action station service include wok stations, mashed potato bars, fajitas, pasta, grilled meats, omelets, crepes, sushi, flaming desserts and spinning salad bowls. These stations are sometimes called "performance stations" or "exhibition cooking."

Cafeteria Service

For cafeteria service, Guests stand in line but do not help themselves. They are served by chefs and/or servers from behind the buffet line. This is a way to control portion sizes. Sometimes the inexpensive items, such as salads, will be self-service. Expensive meat items are served by an attendant.

Plated Buffet Service

Selection of pre-plated foods, such as entrees, sandwich plates and salad plates, are set on a buffet table. They may also be placed on a roll-in (rolling cart or table) and then moved into the function room at the designated time. Because of individual plates, trays are usually used. This is a particularly good idea for formal, German, ethnic, and buffet service.

Just What Is French Service, Anyway?

You may have seen Waiters sailing towards tables, holding silver platters aloft. More importantly for you as a Host, you may have been charged for it on your master account. Professional Waiters are adept at several service styles; the most popular is called "French." However, there is some confusion on just what French service is. It is further confused by similarities with Butler and Russian Service. Let's demystify the styles:

There are two types of French service – Cart French and Banquet French. Cart French is what most people are familiar with because it is most commonly used in fine-dining restaurants.

French Cart Service

French Cart Services prepare food tableside. Hot foods are cooked on a rechaud (hot plate) that is on a guerdon (small table). Cold foods, such as Caesar salad, are assembled on the guerdon. Servers plate the finished foods onto individual plates and serve them to Guests from the right. (This is the only style of service where food is served from the right). Some foods, such as desserts, may already be prepared. They are displayed on a cart, the cart is rolled to tableside, and Guests are served after making their selections. This style would only be used for small VIP groups.

Banquet French Service

Platters of food are assembled in the kitchen. Servers take the platters to the table where Guests are seated. The server, using two large silver forks in his or her serving hand, places the food on the Guests' plates (silver salad tongs may be allowed if the forks cannot be coordinated with one hand). Each food item is served by the server from platters to individual plates. Guests are served from the left. Anything that is added to a plate by a server after it has been placed in front of the Guest – soup in a bowl, salad dressing, sauce on dessert, etc. – is part of this type of service.

"It's so important to have manners and treat people from all walks of life the way they should be treated."

David Beckham

11

Buffet Style Game Book

Because buffet style services are so popular, you should be equipped to strategically navigate the field. Foods are arranged on tables for everyone to serve themselves as many times as they like. Guests usually move along the buffet line and choose what they want. When plates are filled, Guests take them to a dining table to eat. Servers usually provide beverage service at tableside. A very elegant buffet will have servers carry guests' plates to their tables for them. Here are a few moves to use:

1. Walk around and look at all the food items before making your selection. Start with what appeals to you the most and work your way toward items you would like to try, without running out of room on your plate.

2. When dining out at a buffet style restaurant, always get a fresh plate before putting food on it. Returning to the buffet line with the same plate is unsanitary and may spread germs.

3. Never reach around someone. You are likely to cause an accident by doing so. This can be avoided if you wait until the person ahead of you is finished making their selection.

4. Keep the line moving. Don't hover while trying to figure out whether or not you want a food item. If you aren't sure, move on and return once you decide.

5. Don't touch any of the food in the serving dishes. Never use your fingers to pluck something off a serving dish. You also don't want to lick your fingers while standing at the serving counter.

6. Place all serving utensils in the original dishes. You don't want to cross-contaminate items. If someone is allergic to a food item that winds up in another dish, that person may become very sick.

7. When you get up from your table to return to the buffet, place your napkin on the seat of your chair to let others know you are returning.

8. If you feel the urge to cough or sneeze, turn your head away from the serving table. Do not cough in your hand or napkin. Instead, turn your head and use your bended elbow.

9. Even though you are serving yourself at a buffet, you will want to leave a tip. The staff still has to remove dirty plates and clean the table.

10. Most buffet style restaurants have a policy of not allowing doggie bags with leftovers. Don't ask.

11. Only take what you know you can eat. If you are still hungry after you finish what's on your plate, you can go back, after the others have a chance to get their first serving.

12. Don't crowd others when they are serving themselves. Give people plenty of personal space and elbow room.

13. Offer to assist when you see someone having trouble balancing a plate or pouring a drink.

14. Help children and get them seated before serving yourself.

15. Due to the casual nature of buffet dining, it is acceptable to start eating as soon as you sit down with your plate, unless the Host or Hostess states otherwise.

"The point is not to pay back kindness but to pass it on."

Julia Alvarez

12

General Rules to Play By

Do

- Pace your eating. Be mindful not to eat too fast or too slow. Eat together, along with the pace of your Guests. This is very important for the kitchen because they are trying to serve everyone a particular course at the same time. Remember, dining to impress is a community meal. You are not eating alone. When your Guests are finished with a meal, so should you.

- Taste food prior to adding additional seasoning.

- Spoon soup away from you, not towards you when eating.

- Test temperature of soup by taking from the edge of the cup or bowl.

- Be conscientious of silverware clacking against the china.

- Carefully consider your meal choice to avoid dishes that can be messy. In general meals like spaghetti, lobster or crab in the shell, and dishes drenched in various sauces should be avoided. Save those favorites for another evening.

- Treat entertaining clients and other important people like planning an event. Consider all the details and also all the nuances.

Don't

- Don't drink, with food in your mouth.

- Don't look over the glass when drinking. Instead, look down towards the beverage glass.

- When a Guest in someone's home, do not ask for condiments that are not already on the table. For example, if you are invited over for dinner, and the host has steak sauce on the table for the steak, do not ask for ketchup.

- Never, never, never groom at the table. Apply that new layer of lipstick or prep your hair in the restroom.

- Do not dip bread in sauce or gravies in your plate.

- Don't gesture with utensils. When attempting to make a point during a conversation, be mindful of your hands, especially when you hold utensils. It is rude to point utensils in an effort to express a thought.

- Double dipping is not permitted. When served an appetizer or condiments to be used by everyone at the table, take what you need onto your saucer and dip from there.

- Leave items that you don't need away from the table. Cell phones are generally not part of the meal. Unless you are expecting an update on a major medical emergency, silence your phone and keep it out of site during the meal. If you are on call for any reason, simply inform the Guest that you are waiting for an important call and may need to excuse yourself if it comes through. Ask if it is ok with everyone and resume dinner.

"May love and laughter light
your days, and warm your
heart and your home.
May good and faithful friends
be yours wherever you roam."

Irish Proverb

13

Post-Game

Test Your Knowledge

1. Who are your partners for a successful dining experience?

2. What side of the dinner plate will you find your bread and butter plate?

3. When a spoon and/or fork are placed at the top of the plate, for what course are they used?

4. What do you do when asked to pass the salt?

5. What should you do if you will be arriving late to dinner?

6. Is it acceptable to put a small handbag on the table? Your cell phone?

7. When invited to someone's home for dinner, what can you bring?

8. What would you say if you need to leave the table to use the restroom?

9. How do you handle soup that is too hot?

10. At what point in the meal do you offer a toast and who drinks after the toast is offered?

11. What is the formula for negotiating the silverware?

12. Who orders first?

13. How many courses should you order?

14. At what point in the meal should you discuss business?

15. Where should you put your napkin when you temporarily leave the table?

16. What is the silent service code to signal you are resting, rather than finished eating?

17. Is it acceptable to eat in the Continental style in America, today?

18. Is it acceptable to put lipstick on at the table?

19. Who should pay for the bill?

Acknowledgements

Our many clients who both trust us and support their associates and members by giving them Protocol International training.

Corporations, colleges & universities, AAU teams, AD's, social and professional organizations, international business men and women, healthcare companies.

Thank you to our community of experts and professionals that help us to be our best. Joyce Cobbs, Sheila Lacey, TiaMarshae Sanford, Deborah Harris, Dr. Larthenia Howard, Natasha Rubin, Barbara Clarke Ruiz, Zakia Barber, Charisse Payne, Loise Sauer, and Sharon Jarrett - "The General".

Thank you to my family.

Philly, Jersey, Moreno Valley, and San Antonio, who understand when I have my computer in my lap.
Forgive me when I take or make that call I shouldn't.
Thanks for your love, despite my cat naps.

Protocol Business Etiquette Training and Professional Development Programs

Business Etiquette

The Protocol and Etiquette of Polished Business Interaction

Dining Skills for the Professional

The Art of Fine Dining as Host or Guest

Techno-Etiquette

The Protocol and Etiquette of Communicating Using Technology

The Art and Strategy of Networking

How to Work a Room and Then What...

Business Meeting Protocol

Meeting Etiquette and Boardroom Protocol

How to Succeed in the International Arena

*The Protocol & Etiquette of
Doing Business Abroad and Hosting*

Social Etiquette

The Nuances of What is Expected of You

Dress to Impress

Put Your Best Image Forward

Consultations Include:

Briefings on Travel Abroad

*Briefings for International Guests Traveling
to the United States*

Special Events, VIPs, and Special Guests

Mystery Shopping Programs

Customer Service Care Programs

Designing Office or Group Protocol

Divisions of Services:

Elite Athlete Division

Global Business Division

Corporate Division

Children and Youth Division

Special Groups Division

Protocol International Institute

Meet Your Protocol and Etiquette Consultant

Cheryl Walker-Robertson is the founder of Protocol International, offering interactive etiquette and protocol workshops and consultations for today's executives and tomorrow's business leaders.

Ms. Walker-Robertson is recognized as a person of extraordinary talent and ability and is often in demand as a speaker and expert on issues facing today's market. Her client range represents Fortune 500 businesses, government, education, entertainment and more.

In addition, her background including 25 years in sales and marketing, Ms. Walker-Robertson has extensive experience in protocol and cultural diversity. A graduate of Saint Augustine's College in North Carolina, she has also studied under the direction of Dorothea Johnson, Protocol Adviser and Liaison to the Washington Diplomatic

Community for the Joint Military Attaché. Ms. Walker-Robertson is a contributing writer to various trade and business publications.

As an executive with Odyssey Media, Ms. Walker-Robertson develops and implements marketing and sales strategies targeting influential multicultural women. Ms. Walker-Robertson is recognized nationwide for her work with Odyssey Network and is responsible for recruiting women for an unprecedented national networking business retreat where understanding the Rules of Engagement come in pretty handy.

90849277R00059

Made in the USA
Columbia, SC
09 March 2018